THE "DEVIL" HATES MARRIAGES

How so many people allow the devil to interfere in the marriage

Cynthia Addison

Expl Ora
BOOKS

EXPLORA BOOKS
700 – 838 West Hastings St. Vancouver, BC V6C 0A6
www.explorabooks.com
Phone: (604) 330 6795

Because of the dynamic nature of the Internet, any web addresses or links contained in this book may have changed since publication and may no longer be valid. The views expressed in this work are solely those of the author and do not necessarily reflect the views of the publisher, and the publisher hereby disclaims any responsibility for them.

ISBN: 978-1-998394-05-0

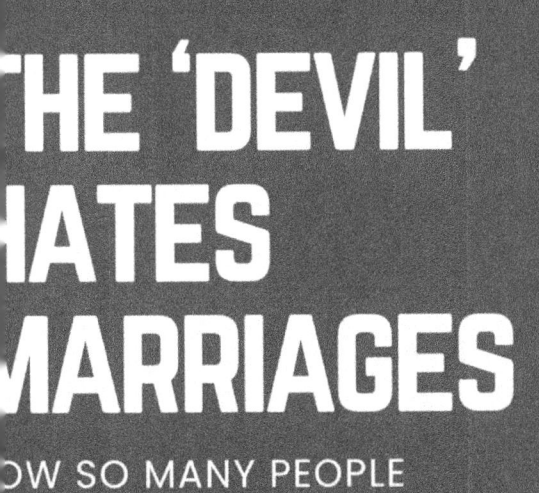

THE 'DEVIL' HATES MARRIAGES

OW SO MANY PEOPLE
LOW THE DEVIL TO
TERFERE IN THE MARRIAGE

Contents

This Book

It is my prayer that, everyone who reads this book will get something good out of it and that somehow in some way it will change your life, your marriage, and even some crazy thoughts you may have or had in your head, that everyone will learn to be patience, understanding, helpful, truthful, gentle, grateful, appreciative, thoughtful, loving, kind, honest, giving, and forgiving.

God bless you and enjoy your reading.

I thank God for everything that he has done in my life, for teaching me and letting me know that if I just only believe, then all things are possible. At eight years old when I learned how to write, it was very difficult for me to read and write. I struggled for a while. When I was a little girl, letters looked like Chinese writing to me. I believed in my heart that one day I would learn. My angel sent from God a lady my teacher, Mrs. Emmerret Richerson, who loved children she took the time and patience to teach me, she was and still is the most wonderful person in this world, and I will never forget her.

At the age of ten, I began to help her with some of the other students in the class, this was only teaching them how to write. At the age of thirteen, I still had difficulties in reading. Another teacher, Ms. Jello Burch helped me. She apologized to me because her class was large with lots of students who didn't want to learn, just played around and called her names. But for me, she saw me trying very hard, and there was no time or room for her to teach me. I asked for extra work to help my grades. But how could I do extra work when I couldn't even understand the classwork. Ms. Burch said that there was one thing for sure, that I wouldn't fail her class.

Ms. Burch looked so sad; I could tell that she was sorry that she didn't have the time to teach me, but she kept her word and passed me. She still didn't give up on me. And certainly, neither did God. I prayed every day and night that I would learn to read like others, I had some heartless cousins who could read very well. The reason I say heartless is because, knowing how hard it was for me they laughed and called me dumb. But I guess they were just being children and just didn't understand, just like children today. I knew that dumb was nowhere near who I was. I knew that God would never make me dumb and I refused to believe it.

You see the Devil messed up my mom and dad's marriage, and some of my cousins would tease me and my sister, saying we had no dad. My older sister would cry, but it didn't hurt me because I was smart enough to know that they were too dumb to understand that my mom and dad being separated doesn't mean that I didn't have a dad. So, I guess some people are dumb in some things, and some are just a little slow at understanding some things. Realizing my cousins weren't as smart as they thought maybe this could be the reason why they thought I was dumb. I realized that there was nothing in this world that anyone could do that I couldn't. God made all of us, so none is greater than the other. All it takes is, believing in God and yourself. It just takes some longer than others.

I prayed and wrote to this preacher who would say all of the time; you can't lose with the stuff I use; meaning prayer; but others had something else in their heads, as for me even as a little girl, knew that prayer works. It did and still does just believing in God alone made me smart. I started learning like you would never believe, I got proud and prouder of myself and so grateful to God. I began to love classes like biology, US History, and math, helping others in biology, and raising my hands to answer questions felt so good. I was in the chorus, the band, a majorette, and even the captain of the golf team. I convinced all of the girls to be on the golf team.

In 1975 while still in high school I worked, and attended business classes at another school. And yes in 1976 I graduated and also started college but while being in college something happened, the students got crazy they started cursing the teacher calling her dumb and telling her that she shouldn't be teaching they knew more than she did. The teacher started crying and left the class, and in my typing class it was a no win, it was too fast and the teacher didn't want to take the time to teach me she spoke fast and just put on a recorder. So, I just couldn't take catching the bus everywhere, going to a place where I couldn't get what I needed, so I went to the office to talk to the administrator and got nowhere. But of course, I still had to pay over three thousand dollars, for a school that I had to leave. But a long story, which will be in my next book. All I can say is God is good and, I am not ashamed of where I came from, I just thank God for where I am.

About the Author

Cynthia Addison divorced mother of four wonderful children, Levi, Lorenzo, Lemont, and Ronnique. Born in New Orleans Louisiana one older sister Loretta died in April of 2005. A younger sister Vanez, was born 14 years after Cynthia after the birth of the sister, Cynthia's mother was sick with a 50-50 chance of living, at the age of 14 Cynthia had to spend a lot of nights sleeping under her mother's bed in the hospital taking care of her mother,

While taking care of her mother in the hospital Loretta her oldest sister took care of the baby Vanez.

After leaving the hospital for a few days Cynthia took care of Vanez but because of how close Cynthia felt to her mother she wanted to spend more time with her besides that Loretta didn't like hospitals and thought, her being the oldest, she would do better with taking care of their little sister. School was out at the time, so it was okay and at the age of 14, Cynthia knew that God would bring her mother through. In this book you will be able to enjoy many stories some are even true.

You will also get to read a short part of Cynthia's, which may help some of you to believe in yourself. Cynthia wrote the book Mamma Said and many other books are written by Cynthia so look out for them.

Dedication

I dedicate this book to my mother who did all she knew how to raise me and my sisters who worked two full-time jobs so that we would have things like other children. And I thank her for giving me life. As many others have done, she could have chosen abortion and missed having someone as wonderful as I am.

And please don't get me wrong I am not judging, I am just happy that someone chose to keep me. And I know that all the children who made it in this world say, hey mom look at me I made it. Now let me say I also dedicate this book to my wonderful children. Levi, Lorenzo, Lemont, and Ronnique Marshall, my father Lester Addison, whom at a later age in my life, I gained a father and daughter relationship with.

And I like others to know that it's never too late to have a relationship with your father, we all just have to learn to forgive and make an effort. For when it's all said and done, one day we all will die. And if we want forgiveness then we will have to learn to forgive. And I must thank my nephew and niece Edward and Laura who always believed and supported me. My grandmother who is 100 years old, Lillie White who we call Mamma Lillie.

As a little girl, all I could remember was every night and day she and my grandfather Clim White prayed, I thought it was all they knew how to do, but when I got older and understood they had 12 children, I knew that they did more than pray. They were the best grandparents a child could ever ask for, I thank them for being there for me while my mother worked, always willing to listen, and I talked a lot so it took a lot of patience and love to do that. Not only that, my grandmother's shoulder was always wet with my tears, thank you mamma Lillie, I love you. And my grandparents Leo and Ada Addison for all of the summer love and support gone but not forgotten.

Last but not least my uncle Laydail White who truly believed in me and my voice allowed me to meet a few famous singers and rehearse with the group called the Gladiators an experience which I will never forget. I have a very large family and just want to say that I love every one of them and thank God for all of the support and love that you give me. But it wouldn't be right if I didn't thank someone who truly considers my brother, who stands by me and has always shown himself to be a true friend and a true man of God. Pastor Charles Martin thank you, my brother.

The Devil Hates Marriages

1.   The Devil Hates Marriage

There was a man who was married and had a three-month-old baby. His name was Larry; he was a very hard-working man who loved God and his family. Larry didn't have much but what he had he was very grateful for it. Larry's wife Shirley wasn't as grateful as Larry, she hated the place where they lived, and the car she had she thought she deserved a better life since she was beautiful and fine. But Larry worked as hard as he could, on two jobs trying to satisfy her it still wasn't enough; he even helped with the baby.

One night Larry had to go to the store, and they ran out of pampers for the baby. As he walked into the store he went to the aisle where the baby items were. A lady standing there whose name was Susie looked at Larry's left hand and saw that he was married. Just what she wanted was a married man with an infant. Susie walked over to Larry smiling and asked, "How old is your baby?" Larry answered, "Three months," Susie knowing that a small baby would have to be keeping his wife up and causing some problems. Susie asks Larry if would he like to join her in having a cup of coffee. Larry holds up his left hand showing his wedding band saying, "How about a ring check?" Not understanding what Larry meant Susie replies, "sure… ok… when?" Larry says, "No you don't understand what I am saying. What I am telling you is to check the ring which means I am married." Susie said, "That's ok with me", Larry said, "But not with me, you see if I drink coffee with anyone it would be with my loving wife." Then Larry left the store with his pampers and went home to his wife and his child.

After walking in the door with the pampers, Larry's wife Shirley is dressed and says she will be back. Shirley went out to the club, and while in the club Shirley met a man named Damien, they danced, had a drink, and exchanged numbers. Damien saw a wedding ring on Shirley's left hand and asked, "Where is your husband?" Shirley answered, "He's at home why?" Damien asked, "Why aren't you there with him?" Shirley answered, "Because I didn't want to be there." So, Damien says, "I will give you a call tomorrow maybe we can do something tomorrow." Shirley replies, "Ok."

Shirley leaves the club and drives back home.

Shirley walks in the door and looks at Larry with a frown on her face Larry asks, "Are you ok?" Shirley says, "Why?" Larry asks, "Why are you so angry?" Shirley replies, "Because I wasn't ready for no baby and I don't like it here." Larry says, "But I love you and our baby, this baby is no mistake it's a blessing from God." Shirley says, "Just leave me alone I am going to sleep," Larry kisses her on the head and says, "Goodnight my love everything will get better." Shirley says, "Leave me alone!" And Shirley turned her back to him and then went to sleep.

The same night there was a man whose name was Bob, married with a two-month-old, and a wonderful wife who loved God and him. Her name is Mary. Bob and Mary were very wealthy and seemed to be happy. Not realizing they were running out of milk for the baby. Bob had to leave his home to go to the store. Bob after making it to the store walked to the aisle where the baby items were.

At this time Susie was still in the store she looked at Bob's left hand and saw that he had a wedding band. As Bob picked up the baby's milk, Susie walked over and said, "Hi how old is your baby?" Bob replies, "Two months" Susie says, "Good congratulations" Bob says, "Thank you." Then Susie says, "How about joining me in a cup of coffee?" Bob says, "That would be nice but I must get home with this milk." Susie says, "I understand, I just needed to talk to someone." Bob says, "I tell you what, I will go home, it's not far from here, only five minutes. I will make up an excuse to leave back out, my wife is very understanding. Then we can sit and talk," Susie says, "Ok I'll meet you at the coffee shop across the street." Bob says, "Ok be right back."

After making it home with the milk, Bob tells his wife that he met some old friends of his, and they are out waiting for him to continue the conversation. Catching up on things that have been going on in their lives. Mary says, "Ok honey be careful out there." Bob kissed her and left. Before he got to the coffee shop, he stopped at the store and picked up a pack of condoms just in case something happened with him and Susie.

Bob makes it to the coffee shop, Susie sees him, and waves across the room while sitting at the table. Bob walks over to her, Susie says, "You made it." Bob says, "Of course I told you I would." Bob and Susie talk for about ten minutes, and then Susie says, "I hope this is no problem," Bob says, "No, no problem, my wife trusts me she would believe anything that I say." Susie says, "That's good I wish my boyfriend would trust me, he's out of town working, and calls me every half hour, thinking I am with someone else." Bob says, "Look at you, you are fine and gorgeous, I wouldn't go out of town and leave you, not for one day." Susie says, "But what about your wife? Isn't she beautiful?" Bob says, "Don't get me wrong I love her but she has gained a little weight after the baby." Then Bob just stopped talking. Susie says, "Go on." Bob says, "I don't want to talk about it." Then Susie says, "Can we go somewhere a little private?" Bob says, "Sure so they left the coffee shop. Susie says, "I have a room two blocks from here at a hotel called 'Nique's Hotel'."

So, Susie gives him the room number he meets her there then Susie makes a drink for the both of them. Susie asked, "How things were going for him since the baby." Bob starts talking about his wife not having enough time to talk to him because she is too busy with the baby, and she is so tired of the baby crying at night especially when he wants to just cuddle up with his wife. Susie being so understanding gives Bob a massage and tells him how much he needs to be loved. Bob agrees and Susie goes into the restroom. Take her negligee out of her purse, puts it on then goes back into the room with Bob. Bob looks at her and then gets very excited because she has all the curves in the right places and beautiful skin, the perfect-looking woman.

Bob wants her badly but knows that he doesn't want to get her pregnant. A baby would be a hard thing to explain to his wife. So, Bob gets a condom that he brought on the way to the coffee shop, hoping to get lucky. He put it on and they started getting intimate. But Bob got so excited the condom broke. Bob feels different knowing that it broke he says, "Oh no! I hope that you didn't get pregnant; my wife would never forgive me if that would happen." Then Susie says, "I hope that she will forgive you if you have aids because I am HIV positive."

Bob jumps up and says, "WHAT!? Why didn't you tell me?" Susie replied, "Why didn't you ask?" Bob says, "Because you look so good and healthy." Then Susie says, "So did the devil until he thought he was bigger than God." Then Susie says, "You see at one time in my life, because of this body and good looks I thought nothing could touch me, and because I knew that most men love the outer beauty. I could have any man I wanted, and make them do anything I wanted them to do. I was in the Church but not really into the Church, just went there to see who was there and what man I could pick up. But one day I met a married man who had lots of money and cars. He also had two children, so I was thinking it would be good and safe. I didn't tell him to put on protection, because I thought nothing could be wrong with a married man who had children. I didn't know that he was also sleeping with other women after he had the children and got this disease.

You see I didn't mind being his mistress, because he was able to take care of me really well, and I didn't have to be with a lot of men anymore. But I was wrong, little that I know that he was HIV positive. So, from that day forth I promised myself that for every unfaithful married man, I would charm him with this body and punish them the way I was. So, you see I am the Adulteress worker from the devil, he said, 'I should work for him', so I agreed because I could never have any children, and non-happiness with a man, I tried and it never worked." Bob says, "I should kill you," Susie says, "We are already dead", so Bob leaves.

As driving all he could do was cry and say to himself, "I had everything a man could want, but threw it away foolishly because of how women looked on the outside, not knowing that she would be so dirty on the inside. I really should just kill myself. My wife didn't do anything to deserve this." Bob took his gun out of the glove compartment and put it to his head, but he could not pull the trigger all he could do was cry. When Bo' got home, he sat on the sofa and the table in front of the sofa, there was a Bible opened to Exodus 20:14, thou shall not commit adultery.

While looking at the Bible and reading, Bob could only cry and hold the bible in his hand. Bob cried so loud, that he awakened his wife. Mary came into the room and asked, what is wrong? All he could say was, I am sorry, I am sorry. Mary didn't understand until she looked at the Bible in his hand and the chapter it was on. Mary said, "Bob what did you do?" Bob explained saying, "I know you're going to hate me." Mary says, "Tell me, just tell me."

Then Bob tells Mary everything that had happened that night. Mary looks at him with tears falling down her face saying, "Why? What did I do?" Bob says, "No honey you did nothing, I was very stupid, and greedy, I am so sorry I don't blame you for hating me." Mary says, "Sweetheart, I don't hate you I love you. And I am sorry this happened to you, but somehow, we are going to get through it." Mary says, "Honey let's pray." So, they held hands, kneeled, and prayed.

A day later Bob died. Sometimes death comes fast, tomorrow is not promised to anyone. Bob left a wonderful wife, an infant, a business, a beautiful home, cars, and lots of money. All that Bob had, still wasn't enough for him. Meanwhile remember Larry who turned down Susie's invitation and gave her a ring check showing her his wedding ring, being a faithful and loyal husband. His wife couldn't take being a wife and a mother anymore for that short amount of time. It was too much for her with a baby only being 3 months. Larry very hard-working man and even helped with the baby, but nothing was ever good enough. Larry's wife was a very pretty woman, and she had all the curves in the right places.

After she had the baby, her shape came back perfect, so she knew that she didn't need to stay in a marriage with a man, who could only pay rent and have a half-decent car. So, she called the man she met in the club, whose name was Damien, who had a big house, two beautiful cars and money. Damien brought her nice things the first week of dating her. So, she was very impressed and excited, so excited she never went back home because she knew that Larry could never afford to give her any of the things Damien could. So, she left Larry and gave parental rights to Larry.

Larry cried and prayed saying, "Lord I was faithful and loyal to my wife, and helped in every way I could. I even brought her things I really couldn't afford and look what she did to me, God, she left me and our baby. I gave her all of me and it still wasn't enough why God why?" God said to Larry, "Now would you be faithful, loyal, and give me all of you?" Larry said, "Yes Lord". God said, "You see I will never leave you nor forsake you, I will be with you even to the end of times." God said, "Weeping endure for a night but joy cometh in the morning." By this, Larry thought his wife was coming back in the morning, but that didn't happen. Larry's wife started living with Damien. The next week Damien told her that he was going to marry her, so she got a divorce from Larry.

One Sunday Larry went to Church, and saw a lady with a small baby praying, asking God what did she do wrong, to have to be left alone to raise a newborn baby. And for her husband to cheat on her and die with a horrible disease, and God said to her, "I will never leave you nor forsake you, weeping to endure for a night but joy cometh in the morning." Larry made his way to the lady with his baby in his arms, he saw the baby in her arms and asked, "How old is your baby?" She said, "2 months" and Larry said, "My baby is 3 months", she replied, "That's good." Then she asked, "So do you and your wife attend this, Church?" Larry answered, "No, this is my first time here I was driving by and something just said for me to go, so I stopped and came in." Larry says, "I just can't believe what the sermon was on." She says, "Yeah how about that, 'The Devil Hate Marriage but God doesn't' He ordains marriage. It was a very good sermon." Then Larry asked, "So do you attend this, Church?" she replied, "No" and said, "I was home crying to God and stopped for a few minutes when a commercial flashed on TV of this Church named 'The Valley Of Faith'."

Then she said, "The pastor said, 'come and get your miracle', it felt like he was talking to me, but I still wouldn't move. Then it felt like something was pushing me out of the house, I got my keys and baby and started driving. I didn't know that the church was in a bad area but I still came." Larry said, "This is not a bad area it is a good area for this Church." Mary said, "But this Church is in the projects." Larry said, "Yes, you see when people get delivered from some other places, they act like they delivered themselves. But when someone is delivered from here, they know that God has delivered them. These people in this project treat each other better than some Church members; I didn't say some Christians, because real Christians know how to treat people." Larry says, "I am sorry we have talked for some time, and I never told you my name, by the way, it's Larry, and no I don't have a wife anymore. My wife divorced me and signed my baby over to me. But where is your husband?" Mary says, "He died. Larry said, "Oh I am sorry." She said, "My name is Mary and it is ok, it's a very long story." Larry said, "I have time so can we take our babies and go somewhere to have a cup of coffee?" Mary answered, "Yes", not knowing they would be going to the same coffee shop where Mary's husband met up with Susie.

They sat and talked for one hour, the morning was almost over it was almost noon. Someone walked in and said, "Oh God, morning is almost over." Then Larry said,

"I know this might sound crazy, you might even think that I am crazy, but I want to ask you something." Mary says, "Yes." Larry says, "Will – Mary stopped him again and said, "I said yes." Larry said, "I'm trying to ask you something", Mary said, "I know, and again the answer was yes." Larry asked, "How did you know what I was going to ask you?" Mary said, "Because joy cometh in the morning." Larry remembered what God said, hearing Mary say this Larry just jumped for joy and thanked God.

After this a lady walked into the Coffee Shop, she looked familiar to Larry. She looked at Larry and said, "So this is your baby?" He said, "Yes, do I know you?" Then she said, "But this is not your wife you had at home, the night you turned me down." Then Larry remembered and said, "oh yes I remember you, but you look different now." She said, "That's because my time is almost up; I can't break up marriages anymore." And then she told him that if he had come back to have coffee with her he would not have been alive today. He asked, "Why?" So, she explained and told him the story, she told Bob after she had given Bob aids.

After leaving the store. Bob's wife remembered what he said the lady he met told him that night. Then Mary said, "So my husband had that coffee and did sleep with you that night?"

Susie said, "Yes, I know because my father sent me to him." After hearing Susie, Larry started shouting louder and louder saying, "Thank you, God! Thank You God!" Realizing because of his faithfulness and his commitment to his marriage, kept him alive.

Mary asked Susie, "Why did you go with my husband?" Susie replied, "I go to and far on the earth seeking for whom I can destroy, and most of the time in a marriage I kill two birds with one stone." Susie says, "you see if a marriage grows in Christ and children are produced it means that children will think about God and that's more souls that Satan loses, and he hates losing. Like I said, "My time is almost up." On the day of Mary and Larry's wedding, Larry's ex-wife is asleep in her big house the house where she thinks that she and her husband-to-be will live forever. But he is out of town right now so there's a knock at the door, so she gets up and answers the door. It's the people coming to get the bed and all the other furniture he had rented and had not paid for but she thought that he owned it. It was very expensive looking and they took all of it.

After this people came in to take back the ring that he had given her which was not paid for either. She thought that it was hers. The next thing that happened, the people who he was leasing the big house from, came in to get the keys and clean up. She also thought that it was his home paid for; they asked for the keys because the lease was up and not renewed. So, she had to get out and had nowhere to go. She tried calling Damien after she asked for him a lady said, "He's not home this is his wife, may I help you?" Larry's ex-wife hung up the phone and cried realizing she had l'ft a good man who truly loved her surely. Larry's ex-wife thinking with her perfect body she knew Larry would maybe forgive her, and even take her back. And just maybe they can remarry.

While riding on the bus on her way to the apartments, she and Larry had lived in the projects she saw a chariot with six white horses. The chariot was gold and white, beautiful, and a band marching behind them as she got a little closer; she looked out of the window of the bus real hard. Then she saw a large lady with two small children dressed so pretty, and then looked over at the man and realized he was her ex-husband, Larry, leaving the church from his wedding with her baby sitting in the chariot with him and his new wife. All Shirley could do was put her head down and cry. Mary and Larry lived happily with their five children. And Shirley realized that she was sleeping with the enemy.

When a man finds a wife, he finds the other part of him. The rib that was used to make a woman, became whole as she joined him.

Gen: 2:22

When a Man Finds a Wife

2.   When a Man Finds a Wife

Male and female have become one whom God has joined together.

Matt 19:4-6

Never Judge the Book by Its Cover

3.   Never Judge the Book by Its Cover

Who would have thought me a single woman, at 52 years old? After raising 4 wonderful children, once living off of $234.00, driving a 1987 Colony Park station wagon, people looking and pointing some even laughing, I was grateful just to not have to walk in the heat and rain, happy that I had a ride.

My daughter at first was also grateful but later began to be embarrassed, not wanting me to pick her up in front of school, and later not even on the school grounds, I had to go 3 streets down from the school to pick her up. My baby boy talked badly about the car and was always embarrassed. But one day the car broke and everyone was so sad, wishing and hoping to have something to ride in, beginning to appreciate that old beat station wagon.

After we got the wagon fixed everyone talked to it as if it was a human and it became part of the family, we named her Betsy after the hurricane because I remember how strong hurricane Betsy was. Even as a little girl, I saw the walls pushing in and all of my uncles trying to hold the wall. Betsy was very strong and lasted a long time, that night it seemed like forever so was that old station wagon, very strong and lasting forever.

Even when I got another used car, a Ford, I thought, ok now we will ride in a better style car, but you know what happened? Before I could get that Ford home, two streets before my street the motor went out. It was a 1997 Ford Concord nice looking on the outside, but the motor just quit all of sudden, and yes, we had to use poor old Betsy to push the Ford home. And again, we had to apologize to Betsy. In 2007 we got Betsy and drove her so many times at a good distance, but in 2009 of March we moved a good distance from our Church, and for a while Betsy made it.

in April Betsy decided it was time to let us know that the distance was getting to be a bit too much for her. So, she began to heat up and we were afraid that one day her motor would go out if she got too hot, so another member of our family who loved Betsy suggested that we leave her with him. And since I knew that she cared about her as we did, I left her with him and knew that we would at least be able to see her sometimes and from time to time our family member who take her for a spin but not far.

Now I am successful and some people thought I didn't want to work, and because of my size, they thought I was lazy and just sat and ate, so far from the truth. Just because I am a large woman doesn't mean that I just sit and eat I don't eat enough, I am always doing something, cleaning, driving, exercising, but never just sitting doing nothing, whenever I am sitting, I am writing or making my little yawn blessed dogs. The reason I call them blessed dogs is because I pray over them before and after they are made. And when making them I put a lot of love into them, hoping that whoever receives them would get a blessing, so please don't judge a book by its cover.

You know Betsy taught me something and I hope that she taught you something, that beauty is not on the outside and you should give a person a chance if they seem to be decent. So, I met this man and he seemed to be a good person but didn't look too good on the outside, and reminded of what I learned from Betsy, I gave him a chance.

But I found out he was messed up in the head, he said he didn't like big women not enough to be serious with them, that they weren't healthy, and that something could happen to them, they could get sick and die. I guess he didn't know smell also dies. And when he told me that he stayed with a woman for two years because everyone thought that she was pretty and fine, but she couldn't do anything right. Then I knew that his head wasn't on right. But you know how some of us women are, thinking maybe he needs a little help and just confused about how and what he should look for in a woman. And since he was someone, I could have a nice time with, just maybe I could fix or change his mind. And for a while, it seemed to work.

16

But a crackhead that he knew said something and it clicked his mind back on stupid.

The crackhead being angry because he thought that he was losing a friend, says to him, "Why do you like the fat woman?" So, he started tripping about me being large and start distancing himself from me, he even got some advice from someone in his family who was also fat. So, I began to understand that this wasn't something I should give another try. I tried to be as nice as I could, but when people keep pushing, you feel like you just have to strike back and I did.

"You see?, he had his last fat word to say, and then it will be my turn. Watching everything I eat and every step I take" he says, "After seeing two women walk into a store," he says, "Look, at least you aren't as big as they are." So, I said, "You know one day this weight on me will drop and I won't be fat, but tell me will you always be ugly? Or could it drop? There is no way of getting rid of the ugly." Then I asked, "Have you always looked like this? Or did it just drop on you? And when will it leave?"

You see first of all if he could let someone whose brain is cooked on crack convince him to look at my size as a problem, then maybe his brain is also cooking on crack or something, or maybe not. Don't judge a book by its cover. We don't use the word crack head, dope head and druggy anymore. It was only the way we felt at the time because we don't know what kind of changes people have made in their lives, so we don't judge any of them.

Can you believe I even had a man tell me if I was fine, he would marry me? He said that he loved me but I had to be fine for him to marry me and I told him that I would marry him if he would lose 300 pounds. And yes, he felt that he was God's gift to me and couldn't understand how I could think that he needed to lose that much weight or even any. Some men are crazy, believing that we can just be happy having a man no matter the look or condition. But we need to fit their charts. Sometimes it's our fault for letting them think that the only thing in this world that matters to us is pleasing them, no matter how we are treated by them causing them to create and judge the book on our cover.

Both Betsy's taught me something. Hurricane Betsy destroyed a lot of things, but things left me and my family alive, something to be grateful for. The car Betsy helped me and my children get to all of the places we needed to get to, emergency room, doctor's office, grocery stores, and even kept us out from the rain, something to be grateful for. She may not have looked good but she was good to and for us. Thank God for Betsy.

Melvin and Dorothy

2.	Melvin and Dorothy

Melvin and Dorothy have two grown children who are married a son and a daughter. Melvin came up from the old school believing all women should know how to cook and clean and made sure his wife taught his daughter. One day Melvin's son came over, talking about his wife complaining, about him coming home late one night and that he had another woman. Melvin asks well son do you have another woman? His son says yes, "Dad I do, but I bring all of my money home." He says that she also works, so Melvin says, "There's no problem", Melvin said, "But if she works, cooks, and keeps the house clean why do you have another woman?" "No, she doesn't cook she never learned," Melvin says, "Can't cook; then son I understand I don't blame you, so does this other woman cook?" "Yes," and very well he replied, Melvin said, "Good son keep her."

Melvin's wife was listening and then said to him, "Melvin you are telling him wrong, his wife works just as he does, and he knows how to cook. At least she does clean he can help in the house and he doesn't need to be out late with some other woman," Melvin says, "Leave him alone, he's just being a man." Melvin's wife Dorothy says, "No just being a dog." Later Melvin and Dorothy's daughter came over crying they asked, "What was wrong?" and she said, "I found out my husband is cheating on me." Melvin shouts out, "Where is my gun!" The daughter said, "My husband is always coming home with new clothes and jewelry and when I asked where he got the things from, he said a friend. I found out that this friend was his supervisor; he even brought her lunch that I cooked." She said, "I don't know what is wrong I do everything cook, clean, and pay all of the bills with the money he gives me."

Melvin says, "I don't understand how he can cheat on my daughter", then Melvin asks, "What did he say when you let him know that you know that he is cheating?" She told Melvin that her husband said that a clean house and cooked food don't help pay the bills, and this other woman gives him money. Dorothy then says, "I guess he is just being a man; all Melvin can do is put his head down understanding that his son's wife is also someone's daughter.

To My Black People

5.   Just Because Obama Is Black

To my black people a wake-up call, President Obama, is not God. There are only a few things that he could do on his own. And one of them is not throwing every other race aside, to tend to his own. What is wrong with you people, thinking that because this man is black, he could address black issues only without including other races? He is the president of the United States of America; this means everyone in the United States, not just blacks. And please don't say he wouldn't be the president if it wasn't for you. Because it wasn't just blacks, who voted for him. Did some of you think that he would be able to just fire everyone in the white house and put you there? You have to stop looking for someone else to blame for your failures.

Did you notice that President Obama is black and made it to the presidential seat? So, what does this tell you? Use this and know that there is nothing you can't do if you want to. This is a great thing that has happened for our country. And I tell you this is the first time in my 52 years that I have said, "My country. I never sang the song, my country, in fact I don't know the song but I am going to learn it. Because now it feels like and is my country, I thank God that before I die in this country I can say and feel that I am truly an American and be proud of it. And hopefully one day I can say that there is justice for all."

So, thank God for Obama. Also, before Obama became the president he wasn't looking for a job he had one. Another thing instead of being like the other people, looking for him to fail and hoping that he makes a mistake every time he speaks. Why don't you be a good black brother and sister for your brother who is trying? Pray for him give him your support and a break, and start speaking for him and not against him. There are some things he cannot say but you can so say them for him. Be your brother's keeper and stop looking for your brother to keep you. I am hoping that it wasn't us who killed Jesus because he came'to save the whole world and not just us.

Robert and Rhonda

6.   Robert and Rhonda

Robert and Rhonda met each other in high school. Robert and Rhonda looked like twin sisters and brothers. One day Rhonda was walking up the stairs to her class, and Robert was walking downstairs to his class. As Robert and Rhonda walked their way they met eye-to-eye with one another on the stairs. One of Robert's friends asked if Rhonda was his sister because they looked just alike. Rhonda smiled at Robert and Robert answered his friend saying, "Yes", and smiling back at Rhonda. So, they went on with this for a while, each day Rhonda and Robert would meet for lunch at school and stay together until the first bell rang.

Rhonda when she first saw Robert on the stairs, she knew that she wanted to be his girlfriend. But since Robert agreed that they would just be brother and sister, even though she had feelings for him when she first looked into his eyes. Rhonda always wanted a brother and thought that it was the only way he could see her, as a sister. So, it was good for a while hanging out with him and his friends. Rhonda was so sweet and innocent.

Robert's two friends wanted Rhonda for a girlfriend, they both really like her. Not only did the two friends like Rhonda, but one day Robert decided to tell Rhonda that he just couldn't take it anymore, that he could not do this brother and sister thing anymore because he had strong feelings for her. But Rhonda didn't take him seriously, she put him in her heart as a real brother, and it couldn't change just like that. So, she said to Robert, "You are my brother" He replied, "Not for real and I don't want to be your brother anymore." Rhonda smiled and looked at him because she still couldn't believe it.

After this every day for school she looked for him but couldn't find him, he would hide from her, he did it until graduation, he graduated a year before her and they never saw each other until years later. They both had gotten married, had children, and separated from their husband and wife. One day Rhonda saw one of Robert's friends, it was right before her birthday, she asked his friend if he had Robert's phone number and when was the last time he had seen him. Robert's friend said, "Oh, we go fishing together all the time." Then he gave Rhonda, Roberts's phone number. Rhonda called but there was no answer.

The next few days Robert showed up at Rhonda's place of business. When she saw him, she was so happy she ran by him and hugged him real tight. He was so amazed and from that day forth they would talk on the phone. She asked if he would come to her birthday party, he accepted the invitation and everyone had a great time. From then on Rhonda only wanted to be friends, but Robert would call every day and night trying to convince Rhonda that she should be with him.

It took months to spend time together every day with other friends, to dinner, etc. Rhonda and Robert begin to spend time alone. She realized how much Robert loved her, so they began to start a strong relationship, and they fell in love with each other. Rhonda later on had a child for Robert, he was the best man a woman could have for her child's father. Robert never missed any of Rhonda's doctor appointments and gave her everything she asked for. On the day of the delivery of his child, Robert was at the hospital. After seeing Rhonda in pain and apologizing to her for being in so much pain, Robert wanted a son, but Rhonda had a girl. Robert asked Rhonda in a playing way if she would do it all over again to give him a son. Rhonda even being drugged up with the antis eager, says sweetly, "Not right now". Robert was so touched, he couldn't believe she could be so sweet being in all of that pain, going through what she had gone through.

Later on, while the baby is now 1 month, Rhonda finds out Robert and his wife decided to try to work things out. Rhonda was very hurt but knew that she had to understand, so she was willing to let go. But Robert came around still, spending time with the baby, going to the baby's doctor appointments, and giving Rhonda lots of attention. So, it began to get even harder for Rhonda to let go. Robert said he needed time to end the marriage because he realized he just couldn't let go of Rhonda. Rhonda held on for as long as she could, then realized Robert wanted his cake and ate it too.

Rhonda knew that this was not the kind of life she wanted to live. And Rhonda knew that if Robert's wife wanted to make the marriage work, maybe he should give it a try, telling him that he had to let go, go on with his life, and try to be a good husband to his wife. Robert would get angry with Rhonda when she would talk about him, do the right thing by his wife, and make the marriage work. Robert would always say to Rhonda, "One day the two of us will be together." But Rhonda told him, "Please just give it up and make your marriage work." Robert told her, "Stop trying to tell me what to do." Rhonda asked, "Why are you trying to hold on to two women?" Then Robert explained that he loved her, but he worked so hard for his home and all of the things he had. It hurt Rhonda even more knowing that Robert loved things more than he loved her. She would have felt better if he stayed with his wife because he loved her, or even felt sorry for her. But not for something that could always be replaced.

Rhonda knew then that she had to truly leave him, so she moved to Minnesota because she knew that it would be the only way that he would let go of her, and maybe try to make his marriage work. But it didn't stop there, even as living so far away, Robert would get in contact with his child, but he would for some reason have to talk to Rhonda, and he would be angry saying, "You left and you took my child away."

But this was the true reason why he was so angry. The reason was that he couldn't see Rhonda anymore. One day he finally admitted it, every chance he would get when calling or talking on the computer, he would make sure to tell Rhonda how much he missed and loved her. Rhonda still trying to tell him to do the right thing and make the marriage work. Rhonda would never stop loving him, but she knew she had to let go and she did it. It has been 12 years and Robert still hasn't given up. But Rhonda prays all the time, that Robert and his wife's marriage work, and that they grow together in Christ with all the happiness in the world.

Rhonda got married again and her marriage was wonderful, well at least in the beginning. But later it became a living hell. Her husband was a wonderful man until his family interfered. Rhonda left to see her sick grandmother, but her husband didn't want to understand why she had to leave for a few days. Rhonda's husband asked her not to go, she asked that he come with her, but he wouldn't. After Rhonda left, she would call her husband each day, and one day his voice sounded strange, she asked if he was ok, and he said yes. But Rhonda knew that he wasn't ok. After making it back home Rhonda's house was a really big mess. So, she asked, "What happened?", he said, "Nothing." After looking in his face Rhonda saw that his face looked very strange, and growing up where she did, she knew that look. It was the look of someone being on drugs. So, she asked if he was taking drugs he answered, "No, no, no way."

So, one day he got hurt and had to go to the doctor working on the type of job he had, the insurance company always asked for a drug test. So, the doctor gave him a drug test, and a few days later the job sent a letter telling him about the drugs that were found in the test. And he no longer was able to work for the company. Rhonda didn't want to keep getting married over and over, and knew that people make mistakes and can change so she told him that it would be ok, that he would get another job. But Rhonda thought maybe they should go to some drug classes so that she would support him and be with him in every class. He said, "Ok".

Two days later he got a job and said everything was ok, and he didn't need classes for a while. Everything seemed to be ok, but Rhonda found out that she was carrying a child. After talking with her husband, he was angry. He didn't want any more children. So, things got really bad, and Rhonda stayed stressed out every day. Her husband's family told him that she was lying there was no pregnancy, and he believed it. Then he started treating her like she was his enemy, they would even go to Church in separate cars. One night Rhonda went into the restroom, the bed was three footsteps from the bathroom. Her husband was lying down in the bed, Rhonda was in so much pain she would scream from the top of her lungs saying, "Oh God please help me," crying out loud. Rhonda's husband would not move. Rhonda didn't know that any human being could ever be that cold and heartless.

After the miscarriage, Rhonda cleaned herself up and drove herself to the hospital. Rhonda's husband never asked any questions. Rhonda gave the papers to her husband and told him that he didn't have to worry about her with a child of his again, that the baby was gone, and to tell his family that she never lied about anything. So as Rhonda knew that he would do, once she turned her back, he took the papers to his family to show that she was pregnant, and lost it. So, when he made it back home, she said, "You can give me my papers back now since you had to show them to your family." He looked very surprised that she knew what he had done and gave her the papers.

After about a week they begin to sleep with each other like husband and wife again. Rhonda couldn't believe the words that came out of his mouth. He said that one day he would love for them to have a child. She asked if he was crazy. After a while, she helps him start his own business, and after making so much money he gets beside himself. Ronda's husband started flirting in front of her, even in Church. He even started taking drugs, he said he knew that he could not high like he wanted to, being around her, and called her self-righteous. He left, then later lost everything, and asked to move back home, Rhonda told him that home is where the heart is, and it is very obvious that his heart left there a long time ago. But she still helped him making sure he had food, and would get up every morning to take him to a job he used to have, that rehired him until he got back on his feet, then wished him well.

And as for Robert, he is still not happy because he chooses to be selfish and stubborn.

What happened to trying to make things work?

7.   Making Things Work

At a time in this world, people used to try to make marriage work. And some marriages did work even through the toughest times. But now in the 20's the marriage is over. If the food is late has too much salt, is burnt, the coffee is cold, someone had to work late, someone called and had the wrong number, 10 pounds added, etc., etc. Small things happen then it's off to divorce court.

Before marriage take some time out, to get to know who you are marrying. Learn to be friends first, listening, watching, observing, making sure the person really and truly loves God and themselves, meaning in the way they take care of themselves, it is the way they will take care of you. If they love God and their self they will learn to love you. Make sure this person has good understanding and communication skills. Check the resume twice for accuracy.

Anthony And Nicole

8.   Anthony And Nicole

Anthony and Nicole were two heated up people, and only had one thing on their mind. Anthony was raised up in a Christian family where the neighborhood and Church people knew his family as, good old decent church people. But Nicole came from a controlling and confused street family. Anthony family even though they were good old Church going people, they still had a whole lot of bad issues and they too were very confused people, not understanding the differences between life for Christ and life for people. They were worried so much about what people would think, and what people see. Not understanding that God see everything, and there are no walls that are so thick that he can't see through.

While Anthony and Nicole were around people, they found out about them sleeping with each other. So somehow Anthony's mother found out and wasn't too pleased with people knowing what her son was doing. So, Anthony and Nicole decided to shack up, but before they shacked up Anthony, being the person, he is always seeking for his mother's approval on everything. After talking it over with Nicole, he went home and told his mother about them thinking of shacking up. But his mother knew that she would never be able to face the Church members, knowing that her son was shacking up.

Anthony's mother knew that he was the only one of

her children that would ever listen to her, the only one who she could always control. So, Anthony's mother told him, no he could not shack up, even though he had other brothers and sisters living in the secret life of shacking, drugs, and fornication. Anthony still knew that he couldn't stop obeying his mother and she also knew it. She told him that he would have to get married; there will be no shacking up.

So, when Anthony told Nicole, Nicole went home and told her mother, it was ok with Nicole's mother for them to shack up because this was the kind of life they were used to. But to hear about marriage, Nicole's mother didn't want this to happen. She told Nicole no, because one day she would meet a man with lots of money and would want to be with him, but if she is married, she wouldn't be able to have a rich life, telling her that Anthony is not the type of man she wants her daughter to marry. But Nicole knew that she wanted to be with Anthony, not for love, but for other reasons. And even though it still wasn't for the right one, Nicole wanted to be with him. So, against her mother's wishes, Nicole married Anthony.

And throughout the whole marriage her mother made her feel bad. Nicole could never be happy her mother controlled her, making her feel so guilty for marrying Anthony, her marriage started getting really bad. Anthony started wishing every day that he had never gotten married saying he felt like he was married to Nicole's mother instead of her. Anthony took all that he could take, left Nicole and moved as far away as he could. Anthony's mother didn't want him to be so far away from her so she secretly arranged for him to get out of the marriage without paying a penny to Nicole. Nicole's mother wanted this marriage over so bad, she didn't even take the time to realize that Nicole could have money, property, and a new car. She even in her greed just wants Nicole out of that marriage. And even though Nicole worked and helped in the home no one thought that she should, at least walk away with something, even though half was hers.

After years passed Anthony became a very rich man but never got married again. His family was happy because they knew that if he had, then it would mean less money for them. Anthony would never trust women, but he would use them for his own pleasure even lying to them about marriage, telling them that he wanted to do the right thing and that he is going to buy them a ring. Some of the women believed him because they knew that he was a church going man. But others knew that it was just like listening to a lot of other lying men so it just didn't matter. Anthony grew bitter and bitter thinking that all women wanted was his money. He was so stuck on what he had; he thought that everyone else was also.

One day he got tired of playing around, and knowing that this just wasn't the way he should live, he began to pray and ask God for forgiveness and to send him a good Christian wife. So, there was one woman put into his life because of his prayer he loved a lot of things about her and she was a woman who love God and also fell in love with him. But he looked for the approval of his family and friends and found fault in her because she wasn't a trophy woman that he could show off to everyone.

So, all the feelings he had inside of him for this woman, he tried hard to kill but even though the feelings wouldn't die, he did. And to please others he died a very lonely rich man. His family and friends spent all of his money on partying and junk. But as for the woman he left behind she owned her own business got very rich and married the poorest man in the church who had a heart of gold and they lived happily ever after.

When it comes down to relationship and marriage, family and friends should just bud out especially mothers. Of course, a good mother, and I repeat, a good mother would want to see her child married to someone who respects and loves them. But if her child chooses to marry someone different, then mom must let them learn on their own. All mom should do is pray that the marriage works, and that they are both very happy together. And if problems occur, mom keep your wonderful wisdom to yourself, and stay out of it, it's not your marriage and it's not your life, you lived and are living yours. So let your grown children, who have become men and women, live their lives. God doesn't make you choose, he gives you the word, and the choice is simply up to you.

When it comes down to Relationships

9.   When it comes down to Relationships

So, it's the same with your children, you raised them gave them the word, now it's their choice. People we must always remember that if we want to be good friends, and good parents. We must love enough to simply believe that there is nothing God can't fix, and if it is or not his will, who are you to think that you need to fix it, you can't fix it but God can. So let him do his job. Too many marriages end, and are broken because of outsiders, family, friends, jealousy, envy, and fear. God honors marriages, but the Devil hates marriage.

So, before you even think about marriage, ask God to send you a good husband or wife, making sure that this person truly know and love God. Then he or she would know how to truly love you.

Amen

Lamar and Ciara

10.   Lamar and Ciara

Lamar and Ciara started talking to each other at a very young age. Just talking as little boyfriends and girlfriends. At age 13 Ciara could never be serious with any boy because of her parents, they were strict they didn't believe in their children holding hands and kissing until age 18.

At the age of 14 Ciara and Lamar broke up, because Lamar saw that Ciara would never change no matter what he said to her. Lamar knew that his friends would always talk about him, having a good girl and not being able to hold hands or kiss. Lamar's friend didn't see the point in having a girlfriend you can't do anything with at all. Because at the age of 14 they were having sex. So, Lamar told Ciara that he was going to stay by his grandmothers for a while, lying because he didn't just want to say it was over. Lamar started talking to another girl who was very experienced, young but had been sleeping with boys. So, Lamar starts sleeping with her.

One day Ciara's friend saw Lamar with the girl holding hands, walking and she went to Ciara's house and told her what she had seen. Ciara didn't believe her friend because she believed he was out of town with his grandmother. So, one day Ciara's friend saw Lamar and the girl again at the soda shop. Ciara's friend went to Ciara's house and told her to come for a walk with her to get something from the soda shop. When they got to the soda shop Lamar and the girl was still there, his back was turned so he could not see Ciara and her friend. Ciara walked up to him, poured her soda on him and said, "Nice grandmother you have here, she walked out of the soda shop."

At 15 the girl was pregnant, but Lamar said it wasn't his. This is what he told his friends. So, Ciara and Lamar see each other again until age 17. They met at a party and started talking again. Lamar was 18 and joined the Army, they wrote to each other all the time and he would even call sometimes. But soon Lamar stopped writing and so did Ciara, they both went their own way until years later at age 20, they got back together because of Ciara's friend, and she thought they should talk again. So, they did, but Lamar learned that at age 20 Ciara still had not let a man have her, because she didn't believe in sex before marriage. Lamar couldn't believe that Ciara had boyfriends in her later teenage life and was still a virgin. Ciara explained that she would never go against her mother's wishes, and that she could never hurt her mom. But most of all her body is very sacred and a precious vessel that would only be shared with her husband.

So, at the age of 21 Ciara and Lamar got married, and lived happily for 2 years. Lamar's mother and sister were wicked and hated Ciara, because they thought she had taken their money away by marrying Lamar, because after getting married he had to take care of his home. Ciara had a very good job, but Lamar still understood that he was married, and need to be a man in his house, and he did. Ciara and Lamar had everything a young couple could ask for. Then Lamar wanted a son, Ciara was not ready for children but she knew she must obey her husband. So, she got pregnant and they had a son.

After the son made 1 year Lamar's mom and friends interfered, trying everything they could to break up the marriage, even voodoo, his mom used it to keep Ciara away. So many things happened, Lamar started having other women, and drinking. Ciara had to leave. But Ciara didn't want her son growing up without a father. So, Lamar promised he would change saying he is sorry, and that he didn't know why he did all the things that he did, that he loves her and wants to be there to raise his son.

After this they had 2 more children and things started getting worse, Lamar would go off for days. Ciara cried asking God why all this is happening, and she don't want to get another husband over her children, she wants them to be raised in a home with their mother and father. But after a while Ciara couldn't take it anymore, staying there for the children just wasn't working, they still didn't have a father, he was gone most of the time, and when he was home, he didn't act like he had children. So, Ciara cut it off after Lamar stayed away for a whole week. It was an on-and-off marriage, for years Lamar made promises and never kept them, and Ciara knew that she had to just let go. So, Ciara just let go.

One day Lamar came by Ciara and explained that he was sorry, and he loved her, and promised to never leave home for days, telling her about his mother doing voodoo on the marriage. But this day was no different from any of the other times. Ciara knew that he meant it this time, but she was just too tired of it all, she just couldn't take it anymore. While Lamar was waiting for an answer Ciara just looked at him crying her eyes out saying, there could never be the two of us anymore. Lamar knew that she really meant it, and that this was truly the end for them. All Lamar could do was sit and cry, also knowing that he had lost a good woman and that he had broken her so bad, there was no fixing that could ever be done.

The oldest child had gone through so much, seeing his mother cry so many days and nights, and even telling her one night, when she had in mind to take her life, while sitting on the floor the child walks by his mother and says, "Mom don't cry God said it's going to be alright." And that day saved her life. The next year the child talks to mom and says, "Mom I know why things happened the way they did with you and dad. The mother asked, "Why son?" And the son told his mom that he saw the movie at his friend's house, and understood all that happened to her and his dad.

"The Devil Hates Marriages"

BEFORE YOU GO

11.   Before You Go

This page I never thought I would write but after seeing and hearing the news today, crying and praying that it wasn't true. That Michael Jackson did not die. But it was, and being reminded of the time of my young age, loving to hear him sing and seeing him dance. It reminded me of so many things, of the fun my sister and I had singing his songs and dancing together, I cried thinking that, this little boy who it seems like I grew up with, never really had a childhood like I did and even though I enjoyed him he only lived to please people. I felt even at his last breath trying to think of ways to put on a good show for people. People say that he would not grow up; I say he had to grow up fast, so when it was time to grow, he simply couldn't grow up. Another thing that I am reminded of is, just as my sister left this world Michael had to leave and we are always surprised when people die forgetting that everyone will die. It is unfortunate that when famous individuals pass away, regardless of their positive actions, any negative aspects, true or not, tend to emerge, placing an additional burden on their families who have to hear about it even while grieving. But when non-famous people pass away, it is often the case that many exaggerated positive stories are told about them, even if they had a reputation for being troublemakers I just wished that Michael would have been able to enjoy his childhood this is something you can never get back no matter how much money you have.

Sometimes parents think that they are doing what is best for their children, thinking that having things is most important but it's not, love is more important than anything in this world and we all need to give it to our loved ones before they leave, there is no later in gone.

I also wish that he could have met a good woman who would have been able to help with the pain, that he had to shy and hide from, someone who would have known how to love him. I think that just maybe he wouldn't have been so confused. And if anything happened in his family, I am sure he has forgiven all before he died. And I hope that America won't have his family suffer through their lives of pain, instead of the happy times. There's a child inside of all of us, all of us in some are reminded of our childhood happy and sad, wishing that we could have had that toy, game, candy, friend, cloth, mother, father, even a sister or brother, attention love, or just a simple embrace, a kind word from someone special. Even now you still want some of those things, but because of what people think you feel that it's too late. For some things, it's never too late. People are always saying grow up, but never understanding all of the things you have gone through and all of the things you missed before it was time to grow. Lots of people are still looking for the attention of their parents but are afraid to say it, knowing they will hear the word of society saying just grow up. If you had the love of a parent, you will never know how it feels, and not ever be able to be a child. So, before you tell anyone to grow up, search yourself to find the child in you, and we remember all of us have a number that will be called one day. But before you go remember, I Love You.

Sara and Adam

12.   Sara and Adam

Sara was a very beautiful woman; her father was a preacher and very strict. Sara met Adam, he was a very handsome man, and a good son to his mother and father. Adam was a son that wanted to go to school, but because his mother felt that he should work the fields and help with taking care of his sister and brother, Adam would be so, so sad.

Adam felt like a slave in his own home, but knew that he had to do whatever he was told. His mother was so mean, and he would be the only one she made do the work. The other children were able to go to school. Sara was tired of working and giving all the money to the home. But sometimes Sara wouldn't even get paid, she would have to keep children for her brothers and sisters and not get paid, then got a job at a store, and had to give all the money to her parents. So, Sara and Adam couldn't wait to get away from their parents. So, they got married, and at first were very happy. They had two beautiful girls, and Adam would come home from work every payday and give Sara his whole paycheck. They always had lots of food, and looked good together. Sara and Adam would take walks down the streets, people saw them and thought they were the most beautiful couple ever, some people were even jealous even family.

So, after a while people would come to him lying, and even his uncle told him that he was stupid, giving his wife his paychecks. The same uncle tried to get Sara to sleep with him, and she refused to. The uncle telling Sara all of the things he would buy for her and give her. This uncle even had a wife but just wasn't satisfied. Adam's mother even came to the house to start trouble, telling him that his wife was careless with his money. Adam's mom is dark-skinned with blue eyes, and his wife is very light-skinned with very long cold black hair, and fingernails looking like a movie star. Adam's mom said that she was a witch, she even said this to his children, and they never forgot. Adam would hear so many lies even from one of Sara's sisters, because she was so jealous of the marriage and life of Adam and her sister.

So, by hearing so many lies about Sara, and having so many painful memories of his childhood, Adam begins to hate and turn into an abusive husband, beating Sara for no reason. Adam is jealous every time a man looks at her, blaming her for them looking at her, beating her threatening her with his gun, even hitting a hole in the wall trying to hit her. Adam started staying out late with his uncle gambling and drinking and coming home drunk beating Sara. Sara felt trapped with no one to help her, she didn't understand what she had done to deserve this, what happened to her wonderful marriage. She didn't want to leave with two beautiful girls raising them alone, believing that the girls need their father, and there was no way that she ever would be involved in another marriage with another man in her home with her girls.

So, Sara took all that she could take. Sara and Adam had brought property to build their dream home, but the dreams were crushed by jealousy and lies. After Adam put a gun to Sara's head, she knew that she had to leave. So, she left. Years later Sara got married again. And again, a wonderful, wonderful marriage to a man that loved her very much, who was willing to give her the world. But again, interference from family and friends.

So, they separated and after a few weeks they were trying to work things out, deciding not to let people stand in their way and control their lives. So even though they were married they decided to date each other, and enjoy spending time together. One night Sara was running late, she had choir rehearsal, and would go by her husband's house for a romantic dinner. While waiting on Sara her husband was out in the backyard working on an electrical part, and someone walked up to him and shot him in the face.

Until this day no one knows who shot him. Sara was so unhappy and always wished that she would have moved earlier. But people said that if she would have then she probably wouldn't have been here today. And Sara said, "if people wouldn't have interfered, he wouldn't have been living in the area where he was, and the both of them would have been together and alive."

Shacking up

13.   Shacking Up

Starts with fear of commitment either from the woman or the man. Remember God is not a God of fear so where does fear come from? Yes, the liar and thief, Satin.

Selfishness

Some people don't want to share what they have with someone else.

Doubt

Some people doubt everything and always doubt that it would ever work for one reason or another.

Faithfulness

Some people know that they can't be trusted, and would never be faithful to anyone.

Honesty

Some people just want to remain liars all their lives. And refuse to ever tell the truth.

Interferences

Some people let others interfere, and talk them out of marriage, because they didn't want to do it in the beginning, and were just looking for someone to blame.

Confused

Some people are just confused and don't know what to do.

Adam and Eve never shacked up; God made her from Adam's rib.

Joseph and Mary didn't shack up even though Mary was caring a child that wasn't his. He trusted God and was obedient.

Michael and Mitchell

14.   Michael and Mitchell

Before Michael and Mitchell got married, Michael thought she would be just like his mother, because she was very clean about herself. But after Michael and Mitchell got married, Michael learned that his wife Mitchell didn't clean the house the way his mother always cleaned her house. Michael's mother kept a very clean house, as clean as any house could be. You could eat off of floors. Michael's mother always wanted to make sure that whenever anyone comes to her house, they would always talk about how clean she and her house were. It was very important that Michael's mother's house would always be spotless. And this is the way Michael grew up believing a woman should keep the house.

Michael always cared about how his family and friends felt about his life, and who he had in it, regardless if he loved the person or not, the only thing that mattered was if the lady looked and was good enough for his family and friends. Michael was in love with a woman who was nice, pretty, honest, faithful and loyal. But one thing was wrong, she was overweight and Michael knew that if he would let his family see her, they would think little of him, and talk about him and the woman. So, Michael had to hide his feelings and accept the fact that he could never marry her. So, Michael married Mitchell because she was fine and looked ok, knowing that his family and friends would approve of her, because she had a body of a supermodel, and she would always be dressed really nice. Mitchell wasn't a bad person she just wasn't a perfect house cleaner like his mother. But she did keep her house clean enough, but this wasn't good enough for Michael, he would always complain about the house not being perfect like his mom. His food would be ready every day, good and clean. But nothing would ever be right like his mom and his sisters do it.

One day Mitchell got tired of everything and put a hidden camera in Michael's mom and sister's home to let him see how clean his precious family is. So, after viewing the video, she showed it to her husband Michael, letting him see how his sister changing her baby on the bed, the baby had diarrhea, it was getting all over the bed and her hand. So, his sister wipes the bed off just a little with a dry rag, not wiping or washing her hands. Then cleaning the baby's nose with her hands and wipes her hand on the apron, after putting the baby down, starts to cook the food, rolling the dough for the biscuits, while cooking holding the spoon over the pot, tasting the food and letting it drop back in the pot, off the spoon. And looking at his mom wiping sweat off her face with her hands, while standing over the pot of food. Then his mom starts peeling peas to cook and not washing them off. Then his mom went into the bathroom and did not wash her hands, but continued with peeling the peas, cutting season and cooking.

So, after this Mitchell says to Michael, "Now you see your wonderful clean family, what kind of food you're putting in your stomach, while going this wonderful clean house eating? I tried everything I could to make the marriage work, even though the only reason why I married you was to get out of my mother's house. I figured I got myself into this mess so I guess I better just stick with it. But you know what? It's just not worth it, I rather go back to my mother's home and put up with cleaning my nasty brother's room. At least we were always taught to keep our food and hands clean at all times, and be careful about what goes inside our stomach. I don't know if you ever paid attention or not, but I never ate with your relatives, because my mother always told me to watch people with houses that are too clean. Some of the houses that are just too clean, aren't clean with their food. A clean house is mostly for show and tell.

Now go and tell your family and friends these divorce papers. And you keep this trophy wife picture to carry around with you so you can tell everyone about the perfect one you let go away."

Some Times We Need To Be Saved From Our Self

15.   Saved from ourself

We can make some bad decisions and choices, and get us in a lot of trouble. Our self tells us we need someone in our life, and no matter how much they hurt us we should just keep giving them chance after chance. Our self tells us that we can change the other person, even though they don't want to change. Our self tells us that even though they say they don't love us; in their mind they do. Our self tells us that we can't get anyone better, and at least this person has some good qualities. Our self tells us that they don't really mean the bad things they say to us. Our self tells us that we can't do any better. Our self tells us that we need to drink and get drunk, so that we can forget about all of our problems. Our self tells us that sex will help us keep the person we love forever, but later that person leaves us. Our self tells us that we should get high. Our self tells us that we are nobody. Our self tells us that we need to fit in. Our self tells us that we are too fat, too skinny, too ugly, too black, too white, too red, too bright. Our self tells us that we should just give up and die, that we won't be able to make it in this world. Our self tells us that we need to be like someone else. Now is the time to stop listening to yourself, and just take a long look at yourself, and let God save you from yourself.

Rebecca And Floyd

16.   Rebecca And Floyd

Rebecca met Floyd while he was in the music business. Rebecca knew that Floyd had lots of women coming after him, she even knew that he was sleeping with a lot of them. But it didn't matter to her, she had her own little plan to make sure Floyd marry her. So, when he made it big in the music business, she would have everything she always wanted. So, Rebecca got all of the people she knew to try and convince Floyd to marry her. Rebecca would make sure she brings him around all of her married friends to show him that everyone is doing it, and how odd he and she would look around them.

So, one day Floyd just got tired of Rebecca mopping around looking sad, and even though he knew that he just wasn't ready for a commitment he got her a ring thinking this would stop the nagging and keep everyone else off his back for a while. But it didn't work.

Later Rebecca her family, and friends began to make this big wedding plain. But Floyd knowing that he wasn't ready for all of this told Rebecca that it was just too much money to be spent and he wanted to have a home and money before he got married. Rebecca was still determined to make this marriage happen before he got rich. Knowing that things might change if he would get rich first. So, she suggested that they should just go to the justice of the peace then later have a big wedding. Floyd saw that there's no way that he would ever get out of this so he just gave in to Rebecca. They got married by the justice of the peace and Rebecca was happy, but Floyd never stopped being with other women, Rebecca knew that it wouldn't stop but all that mattered was that she got what she wanted and knew that no matter what she would be well taken care of.

As time went on Floyd music was progressing and the women where increasing he had three women a week and sometimes more, you see in Floyd's life there were only two relationships when he was in love and he messed both of them up by being a male whore, then vowel to never fall in love again. This was one of the reasons why he never wanted to get married. Floyd's wife got tired of him going out and staying out for nights.

One day she talked to her friends and family about Floyd staying out so much, and they told her since she never loved him, to just be secure in knowing that soon she would be getting paid and they said, "Maybe to be safe you should have a baby." So, Rebecca got pregnant with twin girls. Rebecca was sad about this because she remembered, she and Floyd once talking about children and him saying that if he would have a child he would want it to be a boy. So, Rebecca knew that even though she will be rich she would still have to raise twin girls by herself, and she remembered how hard it was for her to come up without a father realizing that this may have been a terrible mistake on the children's behalf, while crying she realize listening to family and friends on the baby part may not have been a good idea, because she doesn't even know how to take care of one child defiantly not two.

Rebecca got two jobs so that she wouldn't have to be home with the twins. Rebecca's mother babysat for about 3 days, then found that she just couldn't do it anymore so she asked Floyd to ask his mother to keep the twins, Floyd's mother knew that Rebecca hated her because she didn't like how close Floyd and his family is, and wish that her family could be like them, so in knowing that Rebecca's mother-in-law says, "No", because Rebecca wanted her grandchildren nor her own son to come around her, but now that she work two jobs to stay away from her own children and have no one to help with them now it's ok that they come around her. As much as I love my son and his children, I say to you no find someone else. Rebecca had to quit her jobs because Floyd didn't want his children in daycare.

As time passed and the children were a year old they were like handicapped, they didn't know how to do anything at all, Rebecca being at home with them didn't teach them anything at all, all she would do was talk on the phone and watch TV every day then she began to gain weight and buy all kinds of equipment and not use it. Rebecca knew that she just didn't want to be in the house with the twins, Floyd started being home more during the day thinking he might get a little rest. But Rebecca found a way to make things work out for her, she got a job working in the morning, and Floyd even though he was tired he agreed to it. Floyd watched the twins in the morning because the music business wasn't working out too well, he had even stopped seeing women. Floyd started missing his mother, brothers, and sisters, it was like everything was cut off from his life. He even forgot how to smile they didn't even want him to talk to them on the phone.

One day Floyd got tired, packed his clothes, and left, He moved away. Rebecca just couldn't take the twins she tried to find him but could not because he didn't want to be found. So, she took the twins to his mother, Rebecca knocked on the door Floyd's mother answered Rebecca standing there with the twins, as she looked at Floyd's mother she started to cry saying; I have no one to give them to and I just can't keep them. So, Rebecca just left the twins and took off in a cab.

After six years Rebecca went back to Floyd's mother's home and asked for her children in a very nasty way. But Floyd's mother just looked at her smiled and said, "It's ok Rebecca I know that you never liked me, but I love you and may God bless you." Rebecca looks into Floyd's mother's eyes and starts crying and says, "I am so sorry for everything. You see I wanted the kind of love that you and your family have for my family." She held Rebecca close to her and said, "Baby don't you know that you are my family? You see? when you married into this family you became family another one of my daughters, no one in this family ever looked at you as being any different from anyone in this family until you separated yourself from us. But still even when I knew that you didn't like me I just kept on loving you though I was very hurt, and the same thing I would do to my other daughters I do to you that's why I refused to keep the children the first time because as much as I love my children I will never keep them from learning a lesson." Rebecca says with a smile, "Mom I thank you; I know what this lesson is, never cut off your nose to spite your face." And Floyd's mom thought to herself yes and never marry for money but always for love.

Walk Away From Self Destruction

17.   Walk Away from Self Destruction

Some women don't want to hear the word. Women are weak, but those same women don't know how to just walk away. All women are not weak, and none of them have to be, all you have to do is love yourself, then you will learn to just walk away. If you don't walk away you will continue to get hurt, get weak, gain low self-esteem, be abused, and be used by everyone, and I mean people in general.

Love, even though most people want to believe that it's pan, it's not. Love feels good, looks good, and is good. Love is giving not taking. True love is simply beautiful. But there could never be love like the love of God (perfect). See, God always shows us signs in relationships, even before we get married, but we always ignore the signs, listening to ourselves. So why don't we one day just get smart enough to listen to God, and ignore ourselves. Let God and Let go of self.

Deborah and Curtis

18.   Deborah and Curtis

Deborah was a little wild, like partying, and was close to her mother. But one day she met a man, who worked hard and loved being with her, his name was Curtis. Curtis fell in love with Deborah, and married her. Later they had five children, and Curtis found a good job making lots of money. Curtis wanted Deborah and his children to have all the finer things in life. So, Curtis brought a nice big home for them.

Curtis didn't like going out to clubs, but Deborah did. Curtis would just stay home on the weekend, spending time with the children. And sometimes on Curtis's off days he would cook and clean because Deborah would go to school for nursing. Curtis would make sure when Deborah came home from school, that the children were fed, bathed, and asleep. Curtis made sure that her bath water was run with rose peddles, and her food was on the table with a long white candle lit by it waiting for her.

Curtis loved trying to find out, what else he could do to make Deborah's life happy, always trying to communicate with her. But Deborah never felt like talking all the time, she said that Curtis just talk too much. Deborah would leave home a lot going to her mother's home. Deborah's mother would say to her, don't let no man tell you what to do. And she would tell Curtis what her mother said. Curtis would get angry with his mother-in-law, saying, "She is trying to cause trouble in our home". So, he asked Deborah not to go by her mother. Deborah told her mother, her mother called Curtis, and says, "You can never keep her from me." Then Curtis had to do something he didn't want to do. Curtis asked his wife to make a choice between him and her mother. Deborah thought that he was crazy asking her to do this.

So, she in her mind had decided to choose her mother. But something happened that day. God sent a stranger to Deborah, an old lady who she had never met before, was riding in the car with an old friend of Deborah. As they approached Deborah, she and the old friend were so happy to see each other, the old friend asked, "How are things going on in your life?" Deborah told her everything, and as the old lady listened.

When Deborah finally finished, the old lady said, "Young lady, I don't mean to interfere, but to me it sounds like you have the type of husband that a lot of women have been looking for, and still are. He works, communicates, helps in the house, helps with the children, doesn't go out to clubs or parties, pleases you, and most of all he loves you. Please forgive me for saying this, but it's the truth, when it comes down to a choice between your mother and your husband, you made a commitment when you said the words at the altar, 'I do'.

The Bible says, "The husband is over you not your mother." And let me tell you something else, as soon as you let that good man go, someone else will be standing with open arms to receive him, someone who has been waiting. And trust me you will never be able to get him back because the person who is waiting on him will make sure they never make the same mistakes you did. Deborah listens, good stuff you want to always hold on to, but trash you need to throw it out very fast, and what you have is good stuff." No one ever talked to Deborah like this before, but at that moment she realized that the old lady had to be an angel sent from God. Deborah thanked the lady and, went back home to her husband apologizing, telling him how much she appreciated him and love him. Deborah stopped going out and spent time with her husband and children.

After a while the husband called Deborah's mother and invited her over for dinner. That day Deborah's mother understood that Curtis never controlled, or even tried to control Deborah, he only loved her. The whole family got along very well. Curtis went into his room thanking God for answering his prayers and blessing his marriage.

Joe and Carey

19.   Joe and Carey

There was a football player named Joe, who was very rich, and decided to retire at a young age. He had all of the money he needed, but no one to share it with. He couldn't have children but always wanted his son who he would be able to teach how to play football. He was very sad even though he had a big home, cars, and lots of money. He would always go to parks to watch the little children play football, wishing that one of them was his. He never let anyone know who he was; he would disguise himself because he was out there also looking for a wife. He wanted a woman who had children even though a lot of men were running from women who did, he was different, he would watch the mothers and how they were with their children, with discipline and love, because he knew that he couldn't be in a relationship with a woman whose children was out of control.

Every week he would watch this certain lady who had an old beat-up van, she would drop her son off and kiss him, telling him she would be back. After she dropped off his brothers at their football practice, because of them being younger, they had to play for another park which was a distance from the other brother. And just as she said, she did come back. While sitting on the bleachers, with a loud voice letting him know that she is there for him. As he looks up and sees her, he smiles and tries to play his best.

Each time he makes a good play she hollers very loudly, letting him know that she was proud. And when he makes a wrong play, she would let him know that she wasn't happy with it, and then he would try hard not to mess up again.

After sitting and watching for a while Joe decides to ask her name, she says, "Carey". Joe tries to hold a conversation with her but she is really into her son's game, and she tells him that she can't talk she must let her son know that she is paying attention to his game, and soon will have to leave to watch the practice of her other sons, "So please just leave me alone" says Carey.

After 10 minutes passed Carey started to get up and said to Joe, "Mr. I am sorry, I don't mean to be rude but my job with these boys is very heavy and I must give them all the time I can, it was nice meeting you Mr. Joe but I have to go now to see my other sons and let them know I am there for them." Then Joe asked, "How are you going to get back in time to pick this one up?" She answers, "Trust me I will make it on time." So, Joe knew that he would at least see her again that day.

Carey made it to the practice of her other sons, and as usual making sure they know that she was there. In a loud voice she called their names Lemont, Lorenzo, mamma is here. So, they looked up and smiled, they never had any doubt that she wouldn't be there because every week, like clockwork, mom was there.

After practice Carey would gather the boys and their sister saying, "Hurry up we have to make it on time to pick your brother up." Poor Carey would have to drive fast all of the time to make it back and forth, being afraid of getting a speeding ticket something she knew she could not afford. You see she had a stroke a year ago from trying to work two full-time jobs to support her children. Now Carey can only work part-time, and take care of her children. her ex-husband would only pay child support whenever he felt like it, and that wasn't too often, he would never spend any time with the children, not even call.

Carey makes it back to the park to pick up her oldest son Levi. All of the children jump out of the van run to Levi and asked, "Did you win? He smiles, looks up at Carey, and says, "Of course we won." Carey smiles hugs him and says, "I am so proud of you." The other boy says, "Mom we did well at practice" she says, "Yes I know and I am also proud of you guys" then she says, "I love all of you", hugging her daughter also and says, "I am the proudest mother in the world." Joe was standing close by listening, feeling good about what he saw and heard. Then Joe asked if he could take them out for pizza to celebrate, the children looked at Carey saying, "Please, Mom" she answered, "No we must go home I have lots of work to do, maybe some other time." Carey says, "Thank you to Joe, we don't have the time, we must go home" so Joe asks, "Then can I at least have your number?" Carey says, "No, I am sorry I don't have time to talk to people, I am always running with and for my children." Joe didn't push it because he knew that this was something he liked, how so much love was in this family and the children after the mother said no. the children didn't say anything not even a bad look on their faces, like whatever mom says that's it, very impressive.

So, at the next game Joe saw Carey and gave her his number saying, "I know I can't talk much because you have to be into this game for your son, but can I at least give you, my number?" Carey says, "Look Mr. do you see those children? I am all that they have and I don't have time for anything else in my life, I gave them birth, they didn't ask to be in this world and certainly didn't ask to have a father who would not care to be in their life." Carey says, "I will not bring someone into their life to hurt them nor me, so I'll rather be alone and happy with my children, we live in a one-bedroom house and we are still happy with each other, don't get me wrong we have some sad days, but when we look up at each other and know that we all are together, the sadness goes away." Carey said to Joe, "I know that I don't have to tell you all of this but I am, so you would understand and stop trying, so please just let go and let me enjoy my son's game." Joe says, "I understand and I am sorry."

So about 20 minutes later Carey leaves to pick up the other boys. Joe knows the routine so he makes sure right before she gets back, he has pizza and soda at the park for her children, he reaches it to her and says, "I will never hurt you or your children", then walks away. Joe left the park and waited for Carey to drive off, he had a different color car than he usually rides to the park with. So, Joe followed Carey to her apartment. While looking at the door she walked by, he remembered the number on the door.

The next day he sent lots of toys and twenty dozen roses with a note saying, "Please can I take you and your children out for dinner? I promise I won't hurt you." He left his phone number on the card. Carey called and said, "Thank you for the flowers and the things you sent, but how did you know where I live?" Joe said, "Please don't be angry but I knew you would never tell me where you lived, so I followed you and I promise I will never come to your home unless you invite me."

Carey said, "You see, to be a nice person and I know it took a lot of money to buy those things, so I know you are dealing with drugs and I will never be mixed up with anyone who lives that kind of life, and to tell you the truth I don't want to be mixed up with anyone, please Mr. leave us alone." Joe says, "I can't leave you alone, I care for you and I know in my heart that you and your children are the family I have been looking for, for a long time." Then Joe says, "And no, I am not a drug dealer, I worked hard for my money and didn't mind using it on a wonderful family like yours." Joe asks, "Why don't you just give me a chance to show you and your children that I am for real?" Carey says, "Ok we will go to dinner with you, but I will meet you. So where are we going?" Joe says, "How about check e cheese? Carey says, "ok".

After telling the children they were so excited and happy. So, they got into the van and met at Chuck e cheese. Joe gave the children a lot of tokens, so that he would have lots of time to spend with Carey. But Joe spent more time playing games with the children than with Carey. Carey played mostly with her little girl Ronnique. Everyone had lots of fun.

After eating and playing the games, Joe walked them to Carey's van and all of the children looked at Joe and smiled saying, "Thank you sir". Joe says, "You all are very welcome, I enjoyed myself so it is I who want to say thank you guys, I never had so much fun in my life." Carey, while looking at Joe's love for children, seeing that he was really serious, thought to herself, just maybe I should try and at least be friends with him, but she didn't say anything, just thank you Joe and goodnight.

Later after getting the children off to bed, Carey starts smiling to herself thinking about the smiles on her children's faces thinking how she has never met or ever remembered a man showing that he cares about her children. Carey picks up the phone and calls Joe. She says, "I hope I didn't disturb you." Joe says, "You will never be a disturbance unless you disturb my thoughts of you, which actually I take that back, you did disturb my wonderful thoughts, I was just thinking about you and the children, how much fun it was being with you all." Carey laughs and says, "Actually that is why I called; just to thank you again, because I was thinking how much fun we had with you." Then Joe asks, "How are the children doing?" Carey says, "They all passed out from so much fun." Joe says, "You have the best children I have ever seen, and their father doesn't know what he is missing, a man has to be a fool to have children and not to be in their lives, children are the most wonderful gifts in this world." Carey says, "How many children do you have?" Joe says, "That is an insult, explaining to her that if he had children when she saw him the very first time, she would have seen his children, and at Chuck e Cheese he would have had them with him. Joe says, "I don't have children and could never have any because of a back injury, but it won't stop me from loving all children." Carey says, "I am sorry." Joe says, "It's ok, who knows how things would have turned out if I had children because I had some really bad women in my life, so maybe it would have been an unhappy life for them, having a bad mom, but you are one in a life time. I watched you with the children and you are what every child a wonderful loving needs parent. So many children I see have mothers who are selfish and very unappreciative, they don't care how their children feel or where the children are, but you are so great." Carey says, "Thank you, I just want to be everything I wanted my mother to be in my life, I know sometimes I drag myself too hard but it's worth it each time I see them smile."

After a while, Carey says to Joe, "Ok, I don't want to keep you too long and the both of us should get some sleep." Joe says, "Ok, but can I ask for one more favor before we hang up?" Carey says, "What?" Joe says, "Can you and the children join me in service on Sunday at this church I attend?" Carey says, "I am so sorry but maybe next Sunday because our church communion is this Sunday and I really can't miss it. Then Joe asks, "So would it be ok if I joined you and the children in your service?" Carey says, "ok."

So, Carey gives him the name and address of her church. When Joe arrived at the church all the single women's eyes were on him and saying, "OH MY GOD WHO IS THAT LOOKING SO GOOD?" Carey and her children turned around, the children ran and hugged Joe smiling saying, "Hay, so happy to see him. Every single woman looked at Carey saying, "Oh." Carey says, "No he's just a friend nothing more." Joe walks up says, "Good morning to all of the women, and kisses Carey's hand. The women say, "Oh, just a friend?"

After service Joe walks up to the pastor and says, "I really enjoyed the service." The pastor says, "Thank you my son, have you visited here before?" Joe explained that he is a guest of Carey, the Pastor said, "Oh ok, well we appreciate you coming to worship with us", then shakes Joe's hand. While shaking Joe's hand the pastor saw something in a vision, then said, "My son, God says he hears your cry and you will have what you say, your prayers are being answered right now." Joe began to cry and say, "Thank you God", then thanked the pastor. The pastor looks at Joe closer and says, "You look familiar." Joe gives the pastor a look to keep the words from coming out because he doesn't want anyone to know who he is yet. So, the pastor didn't say anything except, "God bless you my son and come anytime and worship with us." Joe while walking away says, "Oh I will."

After leaving out of the Church an older woman was walking fast just to get to Joe, shaking his hand, giving him her phone numbers. Joe tried hard to reach Carey and almost missed her, but the van does not start, so she gets out of the van and opens the hood. Joe says to everyone, "Excuse me please, walks away and walks by Carey asks her, "Why were you leaving before saying goodbye to him?" Carey says, "You looked very busy and I thought you would be a while and on Sunday's, I try to get home as fast as I can to cook for the children." Joe says, "How about we let the tow truck take your van to my mechanic, and you and the children ride with me to a restaurant to eat." Carey says, "No I have to fix my van now I need it for tomorrow and I can't pay for tow truck and mechanic, and you have done enough for us." Joe says, "Please let me do this." Carey says, "You know how I can pay you back, my boys can cut your grass if you have grass, do you?" Joe says, "Yes I do have grass." Carey says, "I could clean and wash for you if that's ok with you." And Joe says, "We will talk about it later but now I am hungry and so are the children, so please can we go?"

Joe took Carey and the children to a really expensive restaurant and the children were so amazed they had never seen a place like this. Carey asks, "What kind of job do you work?" After looking at the menu Carey says, "We appreciate this but this is too high and after all the things you are doing for us, we would have to work for you the rest of our lives to pay you back." Then says, "Please let's just go somewhere else." Joe says, "Carey you don't have to pay me anything, all that I do I love doing it and I don't want to be paid, I don't sell drugs, I really can afford it just like I can afford this." Joe takes out a small gift and reaches it to Carey, Carey opens it and it is a huge diamond ring. Carey looks at Joe he says, "Will you and the children marry me?"

The children looked at Carey smiling and she looked at Joe, everyone Joe and the children saying please." Carey says, "Yes." Everyone is happy a popular singer came over to the table singing a song. Some lady walks over with roses and, gives them to Carey. Joe says to Carey and the children, "We will always be a family; I will never leave you guys." Then Joe apologizes for something he didn't do when they first met. Joe says, "I am sorry I didn't tell you all about myself when we first met, but I had to get to know you first. I am a former football player and I do have enough money to pay for this, so please don't worry your van is outside but we must make one stop before you go home."

So, after eating they went out to get in the van, it was an escalade with a red bow. Everyone was so happy Carey and the children crying with tears of joy. They drove to the church. the preacher was waiting because Joe had already called and talked to him, he asked the preacher if he could perform the wedding in two weeks, and the preacher said, "Yes." Carey said, "No, that is too fast." Joe asks, "What do we need to wait for?" Then asks, "Don't we have our family here? All that we need and those who love us will be here, even if it was one week." So, the pastor told Carey, "God has blessed you, so just receive it, God works in mysterious ways." Carey said, "You are right, you see when I first heard Joe say 'the children' it was like a word from heaven letting me know that he would not only love me but love my children as his own. Many men would say 'Your children or those children' but Joe said the children which could easily change to our children. So yes, what more can I ask for, a man who loves God, me, and my children."

Two weeks later Joe, Carey, and the children were married as a happy family in a big mansion.

The Self Righteous

20.   Self-Righteous and Judgmental Church Goers

On this page, I talk a little to the self-righteous and judgmental church goers. (Stop), now remember I didn't say the Christians because Christians know better. As I was saying the church goers, because I see a lot of church goers judging and saying what they think is right. Not reading the word and understanding what the bible says, but thinking on their own, and saying what they want, even talking about the young people and the rappers. Talking about the paints hanging, and the language. If you believe that it looks bad for the paints to sag then go and talk to them, and tell them why it looks bad.

Explain to them one on one, on how they need to respect themselves and others, and let them know that they are unique young individuals, who don't mind expressing themselves, but there are other ways of expressing themselves. And as for the rappers, have you ever really listened to the music and words, to even try to understand that a lot of them have gone through a lot and just want to let it out, to relieve the pain, from a lot of things that gone on in their lives, that some of you could never be able to go through. And thank God they can get paid doing it, and don't have to be on the corner selling drugs because this is what some think the system set up for them, so that the system can for some reason get them away from society and to get paid for keeping them locked up. It's sad that some people would even be angry, that the rappers are making more than they have made in a lifetime. But look at some of them; they are even helping more people than you would even try. How many of you are out in neighborhoods or highways, or even in front of some night clubs giving the word?

Some of you, even if you do go to neighborhoods, have certain ones picked out. But Jesus went everywhere and you're always saying, "What would Jesus do?" So, stop being afraid with all of the God you say have in you, and go tell some of those rappers that, anger and pain can be dealt with by first, accepting Christ, then forgiveness. Dealing with the flesh is hard to get through things, but dealing with the spirit, is learning to forgive and to love. If you would just get passed the hate, then you could get passed the pain, there's nothing God can't do. If something is wrong then we are all to blame. And there is no such thing as, they are not my children, we are all God's children. He who is without sin cast the first stone. All I can say is, judge not, that you not be judged, sin is sin.

God Bless you.

Alice

21.   Alice

Alice was a very confused young lady, looking for love in all the wrong places, her family would treat her differently from her other sisters and brothers. Alice would take up many classes in college but she would never work in that field, and the jobs she did work, she wouldn't stay over a year. Alice would meet men who would abuse her; this is what she thought she should have in her life. Alice had no respect for herself nor her parents, she would speak to them in a disrespectful manner. Alice wasn't the only one speaking to her parents in a disrespectful manner, so did her sister, even to their poor sick father.

Alice and her sister were very angry with their father for getting sick, believing that life would be better for them if he hadn't gotten ill and had to be in the house all of the time. And just maybe their mother wouldn't be sneaking around with other men. But they didn't understand that even before their father took ill, the marriage was over. It was never a real marriage, from the start the marriage was over, unfaithfulness, lies and mental abuse, started at the beginning of the marriage. Love never was part of this marriage it was only an arrangement and partnership. Alice's father told her the whole story of the marriage and Alice, in her mind thought it would be different for her. So, Alice made herself believe that every man she got involved with she would make him love her. She would take care of her men with the little money she saved up, and would ask her parents for more money. Alice got pregnant by an older married man, and hoped that it would work. The married man began to abuse Alice, and she took this for one year. Later she found out he had another child at the same time her child was born, and even another woman who is 3 months pregnant. So, Alice got out of the relationship but, now she is alone with a child.

As the child got older, Alice began to see the child as a problem, keeping her from having a man in her life. So, she would leave the child with her sick father, until she met one man who didn't mind children. Alice would trust this man alone with her child not knowing what kind of man he was. It was a good thing he was a man who wouldn't hurt a child. Things went well for a while, but Alice tried to take charge of everything. Since she was taking care of the man, buying him everything he would ask for. She begins to treat him like a son, telling him what to do, where he could or couldn't go, he listens to her for a while. But one day got tired of being drugged around like a puppet, and treated like a child. So, he started working and doing things for her. But Alice didn't know how to appreciate it, because she never had any man to do anything for her, she was the one who would take care of them. So, the man got tired of no appreciation, and he just stopped doing for her. Alice, everyday would find something wrong and nag, she would do things to try and get him to hit her.

After getting tired of it all, he starts fighting, and she would love him more. He didn't like what he had become, angry and abusive but it got uncontrollable. Alice would never enjoy a peaceful time, and wouldn't let him rest. She believes that if he didn't hit her it meant he didn't love her, but it turned into hate. So, he knew he had to get out of this relationship. Alice refused to let go until the intimate part of the relationship ended, he started being with other women.

Alice met another man older, who wanted a wife, she didn't like him but she said that she was getting older and she needed to be married. Love didn't matter to her remembering it was the kind of relationship her parents had, and it wasn't too bad so she thought, why not? Alice knew nothing about this man, how real was he around her child or anything, all that mattered was that she would have a husband. Now all she could do is walk around with a smile that wasn't real, and pretend to be happy, thinking each day about how things could have been better, if she only waited and changed her way of thinking, that love wouldn't have to hurt. Abuse is not love; it is a cry for help.

A little something extra

22.   Something Extra

Would someone please tell these women to stop going on these talk shows saying that they are 100 percent that the man is the daddy, and knowing that they have slept with someone else and looking like a plum fool?

Come on, now anyone in their right mind knows that if you sleep around and get pregnant, more than likely you want to know who the father is. News flash, just don't sleep around, of course, sometimes you might just end up getting more than a baby. And would someone explain to me why are these women so surprised and hurt to find out the man is not the dad? Like someone just snuck in and put sperm inside of you. Why would you want to let the whole world know that you are sleeping with lots of men anyway? Enough of that.

WHY

23.   Why?

Why do many people love lies, not too many want to hear the truth. In the book "Mamma Said" it talks about a lot of things that goes on in the Church, things that are wrong. It is a book that is written to change the way people think about the Church. It teaches them about the wrong and the right way to live life. But because so many people are so comfortable living a life of lies, deceitfulness,76orruption, and want to believe that they are going to heaven anyhow, not knowing that there is no turning back at the end. Read "Momma Said" and you won't be sorry. There is a story in this book that everyone who has gone to church can relate to and a lot more that will change the way you feel about going to church and treating those who are in the church.

Most women get upset with me when I go to the bible and speak about men being over women. And a lot of women think that bringing in the most money means that they are over the men. Some women that are married preachers think that because they are the pastor they are over their husband. But the bible says that the man is over his wife. Some women want to be in power so bad they even choose to be a man, not understanding that we always had power, being unique. We can push out whole human beings from our bodies, we can make our bodies do things that no man could ever do. We can work a job, clean a house, take care of the children, and still take care of our husbands, something I have never heard that any man has done or could do all that in one day.

Most Women

24.   Most Women

There are so many other things that a women could do without trying to be the man. We all get hurt in some way or another, but not so hurt that we should want to stop being who we were designed and created to be. Most of the time it's not even because of being hurt, but because we just don't want to be responsible and don't want to do our part, so we sometimes would just take the so-called "easy way" out, and become something we are not.

Everyone should remember that it's not what's on the outside that makes a person ugly, but what's on the inside, which reminds me of something else. What happened to black is beautiful, black is where it's at, I am black and I am proud. Why is it that in almost all of the videos you see, it has to be either someone real light or white? Whatever happened to us being proud? I get really angry when I am always seeing light skinned women on all these videos.

My children always ask me why am I so angry about this, because I am light. They don't understand how I can get so angry, it's because I have always seen people as people and my family is mixed with a little bit of everything. But even in my family the darker children had to feel left out, and some of them would hate the lighter children, because society made them think that light was prettier and better, so they began to hate themselves but take it out on the lighter ones. And in school my best friend was very dark and pretty, and I would get angry because the boys would look over her and talk to me. Some people in my family would wait to see when a child is born to see what color it is. If it's dark there's no response, but if it's light everyone is smiling, saying how pretty it is. I had two dark skin children my first and second.

In my family they would give a baby shower for the women, each time they had babies, but refused to give one when I had my first and second baby. But it even got so bad when I had my third child because they thought me, having a very dark husband all my children would be dark. My third child shocked them and came out real light they didn't give a baby shower either.

I made it a point in my life, to always let all of my children believe and know that they all are beautiful human beings, and not to let anyone make them feel any different. And now all of them are very conceded, but loveable black people. Be proud of who you are, whether dark or light, you are still black and very unique individuals.

Stay proud of being black it is a gift, a wonderful gift that everyone doesn't have. It's sad that the most prejudiced people in this world are blacks. We are of our own people, which is very sad and we are always complaining about others being prejudice. Maybe if we end it, within ourselves it will end for others. All of us are the same color inside, with the same color of blood from the same God. Let's just learn to love while we live in this world until we die.

I Don't Like Them

25.   I Don't Like Them

For the single parents with children, if you have small children, please don't let your man or woman meet them until you get to know the person. Investigate before they meet your children, children are affected when parents start relationships, most are looking for a dad or mom, and hoping this is the one, but as we know it's not always the one. Make sure this person is capable of loving children and not molesting them. Watch how they act, what they say, and how they look at your child, whenever you do feel the time is right for them to meet. Now please make sure right at the time being, you do let them know you have children, but tell them you don't let your children meet people right away, that it would take some time give it about 4 months. And please teach your children to be respectful, no matter how old they are. When the relationship starts make sure the respect goes both ways, and ladies please when chastising your children make sure you have someone in your life that knows how to talk to your children and not beat on them, you do the spanking and let him do the talking, as long as he keeps it on a decent level. And men don't let any woman just beat on your children. Some women will beat because they don't like the mother, or because it's not theirs. Remember I said (some). And to you parents with these older children who think that you are too old to have someone in your life, but it ok for them to have someone in their life and when they feel like leaving, they will leave alone. So don't let them ruin your life, and don't let them run your husband or wife away. Yes, you can love your children forever but let them go, trust me they will.

BUT A REAL MAN

26.   A Real Man

People are always telling us how we should never let a man know about our past relationship how bad we were treated; how unhappy we were in the relationship. Because the next man will only use this to either treat us the same way or even worse, miss using and abusing us. Thinking that we either deserved it and strong enough to take it. And he would just use us as his personal punching bag to let off the steam from a past bad relationship from his so-called perfect woman. Or just maybe from anything that's not going right in his life. And since we are not that perfect woman they always search for, it doesn't matter how much pain they cause us. Until they find another so called perfect woman and they get treated the same or worse. Then something clicks in their brain after it's too late, that just maybe he asked for what he got and deserved to be treated the way he was treated. But a real man will listen and learn from your past. He will hear your heart and feel your pain. He will take everything bad that you have gone through and turn it to good; he will make sure you never have to be reminded of the pain, turn your frown upside down respect you in every way, and please you every day. If he thought in any way of a word that he could say that would brighten up your day he would hold your hand and say, "Baby I will love you every day, skinny, fat, or fine you are perfect, because you are mine." Knowing that women is a gift from God that was put on this earth as princesses, queens, and help mates, better than silver and gold, it should always be a joy for a man to have one in their life and he should always treat her like the queen she was born to be and she will treat you like the king you were born to be. A real man is a man that's after God's heart, a man who always searches for righteousness and you can share everything with him you can tell him everything because, he is A REAL MAN.

Marriage is:

27. Marriage Is
   1. Trust
   2. Honesty
   3. Friendship
   4. Understanding
   5. Secrete
   6. A great partnership
   7. Compassion
   8. Love
   9. joyful
   10. Happiness
   11. Communication
   12. Comfortable
   13. Safe
   14. Growth
   15. Never having to feel alone
   16. Warmth
   17. Compromising
   18. Secure
   19. Marriage is blessed
   20. commitment

A lot of people will say I am wrong.
But who cares?
Because a lot of people will know I am right.

I Owe Myself

28.   I Owe Myself

I find myself in a place where I don't remember so much of the good times in my past relationships, But I remember all of the time that I have wasted trying to keep each relationship, holding on to them when it really wasn't worth it, too much time in my life trying to satisfy others and not myself. At first I was too skinny, and then the problem of being black but not being shaped like most black women and later being too fat now it's being too old. I wasted a lot of time in my life worrying about what people thought of me and how they wanted me to look until age creeps up on me now so much time has passed but not so much that I don't have any to pay myself for what I owe it. I will never be perfect or good enough for this world and I don't owe it anything but I do owe myself everything and I will do my very best to repay all that I owe to myself.

About this book

This book is about different marriages, why they didn't work and how they could have worked, if the people wouldn't allow the devil to interfere. The stories in this book touch on many parts of marriage such as happiness, unhappiness, abuse, lies, fears, and deceitfulness and will help those who are married, thinking about marriage, and in the process. This book even has a little about the author's life and some of the marriages are very true stories, but the names have been changed to protect the innocent. You will even get a chance to try and figure out which marriage was the authors. There are even other extras in this book that speak on different issues like, black, self, and others.

Some people who read this book will think hard about marriage and how to choose before marriage. Even learn the things that are and are not important. And those who are married will learn from their mistakes, it will help change the way they handle things. Some will even learn that with a little work marriage can be beautiful. This book even has a small story that will help some people who have a hard time believing in themselves, helping them understand that anything is possible, and that things aren't as bad as they seem. Take from this book what will help you some things you will like and some you won't, so keep what you like and just deal with what you don't like and pray on it. Enjoy your reading.

www.ingramcontent.com/pod-product-compliance
Lightning Source LLC
Chambersburg PA
CBHW071104120626
46546CB00003B/1271